Book 1

C Programming Success in a Day

BY SAM KEY

&

Book 2
Ruby Programming Professional Made Easy

BY SAM KEY

Book 1

C Programming Success in a Day

BY SAM KEY

Beginners' Guide To Fast, Easy And Efficient Learning Of C Programming

Programming Box Set #9: C Programming Success in a Day & Ruby Programming Professional Made Easy

Table Contents

Introduction

I want to thank you and congratulate you for purchasing the book, "C Programming Success in a Day – Beginners guide to fast, easy and efficient learning of Cc programming".

C. is one of the most popular and most used programming languages back then and today. Many expert developers have started with learning C in order to become knowledgeable in computer programming. In some grade schools and high schools, C programming is included on their curriculum.

If you are having doubts learning the language, do not. C is actually easy to learn. Compared to C++, C is much simpler and offer little. You do not need spend years to become a master of this language.

This book will tackle the basics when it comes to C. It will cover the basic functions you need in order to create programs that can produce output and accept input. Also, in the later chapters, you will learn how to make your program capable of simple thinking. And lastly, the last chapters will deal with teaching you how to create efficient programs with the help of loops.

Anyway, before you start programming using C, you need to get some things ready. First, you will need a compiler. A compiler is a program that will translate, compile, or convert your lines of code as an executable file. It means that, you will need a compiler for you to be able to run the program you have developed.

In case you are using this book as a supplementary source of information and you are taking a course of C, you might already have a compiler given to you by your instructor. If you are not, you can get one of the compilers that are available on the internet from MinGW.org.

You will also need a text editor. One of the best text editors you can use is Notepad++. It is free and can be downloadable from the internet. Also, it works well with MinGW's compiler.

In case you do not have time to configure or install those programs, you can go and get Microsoft's Visual C++ program. It contains all the things you need in order to practice developing programs using C or C++.

Programming Box Set #9: C Programming Success in a Day & Ruby Programming Professional Made Easy

The content of this book was simplified in order for you to comprehend the ideas and practices in developing programs in C easily. Thanks again for purchasing this book. I hope you enjoy it!

Chapter 1: Hello World – the Basics

When coding a C program, you must start your code with the function 'main'. By the way, a function is a collection of action that aims to achieve one or more goals. For example, a vegetable peeler has one function, which is to remove a skin of a vegetable. The peeler is composed of parts (such as the blade and handle) that will aid you to perform its function. A C function is also composed of such components and they are the lines of codes within it.

Also, take note that in order to make your coding life easier, you will need to include some prebuilt headers or functions from your compiler.

To give you an idea on what C code looks like, check the sample below:

```
#include <stdio.h>

int main()

{

        printf( "Hello World!\n" );

        getchar();

        return 0;

}
```

As you can see in the first line, the code used the #include directive to include the stdio.h in the program. In this case, the stdio.h will provide you with access to functions such as printf and getchar.

Main Declaration

After that, the second line contains int main(). This line tells the compiler that there exist a function named main. The int in the line indicates that the function main will return an integer or number.

Curly Braces

The next line contains a curly brace. In C programming, curly braces indicate the start and end of a code block or a function. A code block is a series of codes joined together in a series. When a function is called by the program, all the line of codes inside it will be executed.

Printf()

The printf function, which follows the opening curly brace is the first line of code in your main function or code block. Like the function main, the printf also have a code block within it, which is already created and included since you included <stdio.h> in your program. The function of printf is to print text into your program's display window.

Beside printf is the value or text that you want to print. It should be enclosed in parentheses to abide standard practice. The value that the code want to print is Hello World!. To make sure that printf to recognize that you want to print a string and display the text properly, it should be enclosed inside double quotation marks.

By the way, in programming, a single character is called a character while a sequence of characters is called a string.

Escape Sequence

You might have noticed that the sentence is followed by a \n. In C, \n means new line. Since your program will have problems if you put a new line or press enter on the value of the printf, it is best to use its text equivalent or the escape sequence of the new line.

By the way, the most common escape sequences used in C are:

\t = tab

\f = new page

\r = carriage return

\b = backspace

\v = vertical tab

Semicolons

After the last parenthesis, a semicolon follows. And if you look closer, almost every line of code ends with it. The reasoning behind that is that the semicolon acts as an indicator that it is the end of the line of code or command. Without it, the compiler will think that the following lines are included in the printf function. And if that happens, you will get a syntax error.

Getchar()

Next is the getchar() function. Its purpose is to receive user input from the keyboard. Many programmers use it as a method on pausing a program and letting the program wait for the user to interact with it before it executes the next line of code. To make the program move through after the getchar() function, the user must press the enter key.

In the example, if you compile or run it without getchar(), the program will open the display or the console, display the text, and then immediately close. Without the break provided by the getchar() function, the computer will execute those commands instantaneously. And the program will open and close so fast that you will not be able to even see the Hello World text in the display.

Return Statement

The last line of code in the function is return 0. The return statement is essential in function blocks. When the program reaches this part, the return statement will tell the program its value. Returning the 0 value will make the program interpret that the function or code block that was executed successfully.

And at the last line of the example is the closing curly brace. It signifies that the program has reached the end of the function.

It was not that not hard, was it? With that example alone, you can create simple programs that can display text. Play around with it a bit and familiarize yourself with C's basic syntax.

Chapter 2: Basic Input Output

After experimenting with what you learned in the previous chapter, you might have realized that it was not enough. It was boring. And just displaying what you typed in your program is a bit useless.

This time, this chapter will teach you how to create a program that can interact with the user. Check this code example:

```c
#include <stdio.h>

int main()

{

        int number_container;

        printf( "Enter any number you want! " );

        scanf( "%d", &number_container );

        printf( "The number you entered is %d", number_container );

        getchar();

        return 0;

}
```

Variables

You might have noticed the int number_container part in the first line of the code block. int number_container is an example of variable declaration. To declare a variable in C, you must indicate the variable type first, and then the name of the variable name.

In the example, int was indicated as the variable or data type, which means the variable is an integer. There are other variable types in C such as float for floating-point numbers, char for characters, etc. Alternatively, the name number_container was indicated as the variable's name or identifier.

Variables are used to hold values throughout the program and code blocks. The programmer can let them assign a value to it and retrieve its value when it is needed.

For example:

int number_container;

number_container = 3;

printf ("The variables value is %d", number_container);

In that example, the first line declared that the program should create an integer variable named number_container. The second line assigned a value to the variable. And the third line makes the program print the text together with the value of the variable. When executed, the program will display:

The variables value is 3

You might have noticed the %d on the printf line on the example. The %d part indicates that the next value that will be printed will be an integer. Also, the quotation on the printf ended after %d. Why is that?

In order to print the value of a variable, it must be indicated with the double quotes. If you place double quotes on the variables name, the compiler will treat it as a literal string. If you do this:

int number_container;

number_container = 3;

printf ("The variables value is number_container");

The program will display:

The variables value is number_container

By the way, you can also use %i as a replacement for %d.

Assigning a value to a variable is simple. Just like in the previous example, just indicate the name of variable, follow it with an equal sign, and declare its value.

When creating variables, you must make sure that each variable will have unique names. Also, the variables should never have the same name as functions. In addition, you can declare multiple variables in one line by using commas. Below is an example:

int first_variable, second_variable, third_variable;

Those three variables will be int type variables. And again, never forget to place a semicolon after your declaration.

When assigning a value or retrieving the value of a variable, make sure that you declare its existence first. If not, the compiler will return an error since it will try to access something that does not exist yet.

Scanf()

In the first example in this chapter, you might have noticed the scanf function. The scanf function is also included in the <stdio.h>. Its purpose is to retrieve text user input from the user.

After the program displays the 'Enter any number you want' text, it will proceed in retrieving a number from the user. The cursor will be appear after the text since the new line escape character was no included in the printf.

The cursor will just blink and wait for the user to enter any characters or numbers. To let the program get the number the user typed and let it proceed to the next line of code, he must press the Enter key. Once he does that, the program will display the text 'The number you entered is' and the value of the number the user inputted a while ago.

To make the scanf function work, you must indicate the data type it needs to receive and the location of the variable where the value that scanf will get will be stored. In the example:

scanf("%d", &number_container);

The first part "%d" indicates that the scanf function must retrieve an integer. On the other hand, the next part indicates the location of the variable. You must have noticed the ampersand placed in front of the variable's name. The ampersand retrieves the location of the variable and tells it to the function.

Unlike the typical variable value assignment, scanf needs the location of the variable instead of its name alone. Due to that, without the ampersand, the function will not work.

Math or Arithmetic Operators

Aside from simply giving number variables with values by typing a number, you can assign values by using math operators. In C, you can add, subtract, multiply, and divide numbers and assign the result to variables directly. For example:

int sum;

sum = 1 + 2;

If you print the value of sum, it will return a 3, which is the result of the addition of 1 and 2. By the way, the + sign is for addition, - for subtraction, * for multiplication, and / for division.

With the things you have learned as of now, you can create a simple calculator program. Below is an example code:

```c
#include <stdio.h>

int main()

{

        int first_addend, second_addend, sum;

        printf( "Enter the first addend! " );

        scanf( "%d", &first_addend );

        printf( "\nEnter the second addend! " );

        scanf( "%d", &second_addend );

        sum = first_addend + second_addend;

        printf( "The sum of the two numbers is %d", sum );

        getchar();

        return 0;

}
```

Chapter 3: Conditional Statements

The calculator program seems nice, is it not? However, the previous example limits you on creating programs that only uses one operation, which is a bit disappointing. Well, in this chapter, you can improve that program with the help of if or conditional statements. And of course, learning this will improve your overall programming skills. This is the part where you will be able to make your program 'think'.

'If' statements can allow you to create branches in your code blocks. Using them allows you to let the program think and perform specific functions or actions depending on certain variables and situations. Below is an example:

```
#include <stdio.h>

int main()

{

        int some_number;

        printf( "Welcome to Guess the Magic Number program. \n" );

        printf( "Guess the magic number to win. \n" );

        printf( "Type the magic number and press Enter: " );

        scanf( "%d", &some_number );

        if ( some_number == 3 ) {

                printf( "You guessed the right number! " );

        }

        getchar();

        return 0;

}
```

In the example, the if statement checked if the value of the variable some_number is equal to number 3. In case the user entered the number 3 on the program, the comparison between the variable some_number and three will return TRUE since the value of some_number 3 is true. Since the value that the if statement received was TRUE, then it will process the code block below it. And the result will be:

You guessed the right number!

If the user input a number other than three, the comparison will return a FALSE value. If that happens, the program will skip the code block in the if statement and proceed to the next line of code after the if statement's code block.

By the way, remember that you need to use the curly braces to enclosed the functions that you want to happen in case your if statement returns TRUE. Also, when inserting if statement, you do not need to place a semicolon after the if statement or its code block's closing curly brace. However, you will still need to place semicolons on the functions inside the code blocks of your if statements.

TRUE and FALSE

The if statement will always return TRUE if the condition is satisfied. For example, the condition in the if statement is $10 > 2$. Since 10 is greater than 2, then it is true. On the other hand, the if statement will always return FALSE if the condition is not satisfied. For example, the condition in the if statement is $5 < 5$. Since 5 is not less than 5, then the statement will return a FALSE.

Note that if statements only return two results: TRUE and FALSE. In computer programming, the number equivalent to TRUE is any nonzero number. In some cases, it is only the number 1. On the other hand, the number equivalent of FALSE is zero.

Operators

Also, if statements use comparison, Boolean, or relational and logical operators. Some of those operators are:

== – equal to

!= – not equal to

> – greater than

< – less than

>= – greater than or equal to

<= – less than or equal to

Else Statement

There will be times that you would want your program to do something else in case your if statement return FALSE. And that is what the else statement is for. Check the example below:

```c
#include <stdio.h>
int main()
{
        int some_number;
        printf( "Welcome to Guess the Magic Number program. \n" );
        printf( "Guess the magic number to win. \n" );
        printf( "Type the magic number and press Enter: " );
        scanf( "%d", &some_number );
        if ( some_number == 3 ) {
                printf( "You guessed the right number! " );
```

```
}

else {

        printf( "Sorry. That is the wrong number" );

}

getchar();

return 0;

}
```

If ever the if statement returns FALSE, the program will skip next to the else statement immediately. And since the if statement returns FALSE, it will immediately process the code block inside the else statement.

For example, if the number the user inputted on the program is 2, the if statement will return a FALSE. Due to that, the else statement will be processed, and the program will display:

Sorry. That is the wrong number

On the other hand, if the if statement returns TRUE, it will process the if statement's code block, but it will bypass all the succeeding else statements below it.

Else If

If you want more conditional checks on your program, you will need to take advantage of else if. Else if is a combination of the if and else statement. It will act like an else statement, but instead of letting the program execute the code block below it, it will perform another check as if it was an if statement. Below is an example:

```c
#include <stdio.h>

int main()
{
    int some_number;
    printf( "Welcome to Guess the Magic Number program. \n" );
    printf( "Guess the magic number to win. \n" );
    printf( "Type the magic number and press Enter: " );
    scanf( "%d", &some_number );
    if ( some_number == 3 ) {
        printf( "You guessed the right number! " );
    }
    else if ( some_number > 3 ){
        printf( "Your guess is too high!" );
    }
    else {
        printf( "Your guess is too low!" );
    }
    getchar();
    return 0;
}
```

In case the if statement returns FALSE, the program will evaluate the else if statement. If it returns TRUE, it will execute its code block and ignore the following else statements. However, if it is FALSE, it will proceed on the last else statement, and execute its code block. And just like before, if the first if statement returns true, it will disregard the following else and else if statements.

In the example, if the user inputs 3, he will get the You guessed the right number message. If the user inputs 4 or higher, he will get the Your guess is too high message. And if he inputs any other number, he will get a Your guess is too low message since any number aside from 3 and 4 or higher is automatically lower than 3.

With the knowledge you have now, you can upgrade the example calculator program to handle different operations. Look at the example and study it:

```
#include <stdio.h>
int main()
{
        int first_number, second_number, result, operation;
        printf( "Enter the first number: " );
        scanf( "%d", &first_number );
        printf( "\nEnter the second number: " );
        scanf( "%d", &second_number );
        printf ( "What operation would you like to use? \n" );
        printf ( "Enter 1 for addition. \n" );
        printf ( "Enter 2 for subtraction. \n" );
        printf ( "Enter 3 for multiplication. \n" );
        printf ( "Enter 4 for division. \n" );
```

```c
scanf( "%d", &operation );

if ( operation == 1 ) {

        result = first_number + second_number;

        printf( "The sum is %d", result );

}

else if ( operation == 2 ){

        result = first_number - second_number;

        printf( "The difference is %d", result );

}

else if ( operation == 3 ){

        result = first_number * second_number;

        printf( "The product is %d", result );

}

else if ( operation == 4 ){

        result = first_number / second_number;

        printf( "The quotient is %d", result );

}

else {

        printf( "You have entered an invalid choice." );

}

getchar();

return 0;

}
```

Chapter 4: Looping in C

The calculator's code is getting better, right? As of now, it is possible that you are thinking about the programs that you could create with the usage of the conditional statements.

However, as you might have noticed in the calculator program, it seems kind of painstaking to use. You get to only choose one operation every time you run the program. When the calculation ends, the program closes. And that can be very annoying and unproductive.

To solve that, you must create loops in the program. Loops are designed to let the program execute some of the functions inside its code blocks. It effectively eliminates the need to write some same line of codes. It saves the time of the programmer and it makes the program run more efficiently.

There are four different ways in creating a loop in C. In this chapter, two of the only used and simplest loop method will be discussed. To grasp the concept of looping faster, check the example below:

```
#include <stdio.h>

int main()

{

        int some_number;

        int guess_result;

        guess_result = 0;


        printf( "Welcome to Guess the Magic Number program. \n" );

        printf( "Guess the magic number to win. \n" );

        printf( "You have unlimited chances to guess the number. \n" );
```

```c
while ( guess_result == 0 ) {

        printf( "Guess the magic number: " );
        scanf( "%d", &some_number );
        if ( some_number == 3 ) {
                printf( "You guessed the right number! \n" );
                guess_result = 1;
        }
        else if ( some_number > 3 ){
                printf( "Your guess is too high! \n" );
                guess_result = 0;
        }
        else {
                printf( "Your guess is too low! \n" );
                guess_result = 0;
        }
}
printf( "Thank you for playing. Press Enter to exit this program." );
getchar();
return 0;
}
```

While Loop

In this example, the while loop function was used. The while loop allows the program to execute the code block inside it as long as the condition is met or the argument in it returns TRUE. It is one of the simplest loop function in C. In the example, the condition that the while loop requires is that the guess_result variable should be equal to 0.

As you can see, in order to make sure that the while loop will start, the value of the guess_result variable was set to 0.

If you have not noticed it yet, you can actually nest code blocks within code blocks. In this case, the code block of the if and else statements were inside the code block of the while statement.

Anyway, every time the code reaches the end of the while statement and the guess_result variable is set to 0, it will repeat itself. And to make sure that the program or user experience getting stuck into an infinite loop, a safety measure was included.

In the example, the only way to escape the loop is to guess the magic number. If the if statement within the while code block was satisfied, its code block will run. In that code block, a line of code sets the variable guess_result's value to 1. This effectively prevent the while loop from running once more since the guess_result's value is not 0 anymore, which makes the statement return a FALSE.

Once that happens, the code block of the while loop and the code blocks inside it will be ignored. It will skip to the last printf line, which will display the end program message 'Thank you for playing. Press Enter to exit this program'.

For Loop

The for loop is one of the most handy looping function in C. And its main use is to perform repetitive commands on a set number of times. Below is an example of its use:

```c
#include <stdio.h>

int main()

{
        int some_number;

        int x;

        int y;


        printf( "Welcome to Guess the Magic Number program. \n" );

        printf( "Guess the magic number to win. \n" );

        printf( "You have only three chance of guessing. \n" );

        printf( "If you do not get the correct answer after guessing three times. \n"
);

        printf( "This program will be terminated. \n" );


        for (x = 0; x < 3; x++) {

                y = 3 - x;

                printf( "The number of guesses that you have left is: %d", y );

                printf( "\nGuess the magic number: " );

                scanf( "%d", &some_number );

                if ( some_number == 3 ) {

                        printf( "You guessed the right number! \n" );

                        x = 4;

                }

                else if ( some_number > 3 ){
```

```
            printf( "Your guess is too high! \n " );

      }

      else {

            printf( "Your guess is too low! \n " );

      }

}

printf( "Press the Enter button to close this program. \n" );

getchar();

getchar();

return 0;

}
```

The for statement's argument section or part requires three things. First, the initial value of the variable that will be used. In this case, the example declared that x = 0. Second, the condition. In the example, the for loop will run until x has a value lower than 3. Third, the variable update line. Every time the for loop loops, the variable update will be executed. In this case, the variable update that will be triggered is x++.

Increment and Decrement Operators

By the way, x++ is a variable assignment line. The x is the variable and the ++ is an increment operator. The function of an increment operator is to add 1 to the variable where it was placed. In this case, every time the program reads x++, the program will add 1 to the variable x. If x has a value of 10, the increment operator will change variable x's value to 11.

On the other hand, you can also use the decrement operator instead of the increment operator. The decrement operator is done by place -- next to a variable. Unlike the increment operator, the decrement subtracts 1 to its operand.

Just like the while loop, the for loop will run as long as its condition returns TRUE. However, the for loop has a built in safety measure and variable declaration. You do not need to declare the value needed for its condition outside the statement. And the safety measure to prevent infinite loop is the variable update. However, it does not mean that it will be automatically immune to infinite loops. Poor programming can lead to it. For example:

```
for (x = 1; x > 1; x++) {

        /* Insert Code Block Here */

}
```

In this example, the for loop will enter into an infinite loop unless a proper means of escape from the loop is coded inside its code block.

The structure of the for loop example is almost the same with while loop. The only difference is that the program is set to loop for only three times. In this case, it only allows the user to guess three times or until the value of variable x does not reach 3 or higher.

Every time the user guesses wrong, the value of x is incremented, which puts the loop closer in ending. However, in case the user guesses right, the code block of the if statement assigns a value higher than 3 to variable x in order to escape the loop and end the program.

Conclusion

Thank you again for purchasing this book!

I hope this book was able to help you to learn the basics of C programming. The next step is to learn the other looping methods, pointers, arrays, strings, command line arguments, recursion, and binary trees.

Finally, if you enjoyed this book, please take the time to share your thoughts and post a review on Amazon. We do our best to reach out to readers and provide the best value we can. Your positive review will help us achieve that. It'd be greatly appreciated!

Thank you and good luck!

Book 2

Ruby Programming Professional Made Easy

BY SAM KEY

Expert Ruby Programming Language Success in a Day for any Computer User

Programming Box Set #9: C Programming Success in a Day & Ruby Programming Professional Made Easy

Table Of Contents

Introduction

I want to thank you and congratulate you for purchasing the book, *"Professional Ruby Programming Made Easy: Expert Ruby Programming Language Success in a Day for Any Computer User!"*

This book contains proven steps and strategies on how to write basic lines of code in Ruby. This is especially made for amateur programmers with little to no experience in coding.

Ruby is a programming language which people think is ideal for newbies in the programming field. Congratulations on choosing this programming language. In this book, you will be introduced to all the fundamental aspects of coding in Ruby.

This book will give you a huge boost in your programming skills. However, it is also important to quickly supplement yourself with advanced Ruby tutorials after you are done with this book to retain the knowledge you gain from it.

Thanks again for purchasing this book, I hope you enjoy it!

Chapter 1: Setting Up

This book will assume that you are a bit familiar with computer programming and have made a few lines of codes in some languages. Also, from time to time, the book will provide further explanation of terms and methods that can easily confuse new programmers. In case you encounter a foreign term in the discussion, just take note of it since it and other such terms will be discussed later.

Before anything else, get the latest stable version of Ruby from the web. As of this writing, Ruby's stable version is 2.1.5.

Go to https://www.ruby-lang.org/en/documentation/installation/. In there, you can get the right installer package for the operating system that your computer is running on.

Be mindful of what you are going to download. Many people tend to download the source code of Ruby instead of the installation packages.

Take note of the location or directory where you will install Ruby. Once you are done with the installation, open Ruby's interactive shell.

For people who are using a computer running on Windows, you will find the interactive interpreter inside the bin folder located inside your Ruby installation folder. The file is named irb.bat. If you have installed Ruby using the default location, the interactive shell will be located at: "c:\Ruby21\bin\irb.bat".

What is the interactive shell anyway? In Ruby, you can program using two modes: the interactive mode and the programming mode.

Ruby's Interactive Mode

The interactive mode is an environment wherein Ruby will provide immediate feedback in every line of code or statement you type in to it. It is an ideal environment where new Ruby programmers can test and experiment with codes quickly. You will be using this mode in most parts of this book.

The interactive mode or shell will appear like a typical console or command prompt. In the shell, you should be familiar with two things. First is the cursor. Second is the prompt.

The cursor indicates where you can type or if you can type anything. In the interpreter shell, you can use overtype mode on this by pressing the insert key on your keyboard. You can return to insert mode by pressing the insert key again.

The prompt will look like this: irb(main):001:0>. If this prompt is on, it means that Ruby is ready to accept a line of code or statement from you. For now, type a letter a in the prompt and press the Enter key. The shell or interpreter will move the cursor, show a bunch of text, and display the prompt once again:

irb(main):001:0> a
NameError: undefined local variable or method 'a' for main:Object
        from (irb):1
        from C:/Ruby21/bin/irb:11:in '<main>'
irb(main):002:0>

This time, type "a" on the shell and then press the Enter key. Instead of an error, you have received => "a". Now, type "1" without the quotes. Just like before, the interpreter just provided you with a reply containing the number you entered.

Why does the letter a without the quotes returned an error? As you can see, Ruby provided you with an error message when you just entered the letter a without quotes. In Ruby, characters enclosed in double or single quotes are treated differently.

In the case of the letter a, Ruby understood that when you input "a" with the quotes, you meant that you are inputting the letter a. On the other hand, Ruby thought of something else when you input the letter a without the quotes, which will be discussed later.

You will receive error messages like the one before or other variations of it if you input something that violates Ruby's syntax or something that is impossible to be evaluated or executed by the interpreter. In simple terms, Ruby will provide you notifications like that if it does not understand what you said or cannot do what you commanded.

Now, type "1 + 1", without the double quotes, and press the Enter key. Instead of an error, you will receive this instead:
=> 2

Every time you press the Enter key, the shell check the command or statement you created. If it does not violate the syntax, it will proceed on checking if every word and symbols you placed make sense. Once the statement passes that check, it will evaluate and execute the statement and provide a result or feedback.

In this case, Ruby has evaluated the addition operation you commanded and replied the number 2, which is the sum of 1 + 1. Just before the number 2, an equal sign and "greater than" sign were placed. Those two denotes that the next value is the result of the statement you entered.

You might have thought that Ruby can be a good calculator. Indeed it is, but statements like "1 + 1" and "a" are only processed like that in the interactive mode of Ruby. If you include a line like that when coding in programming mode, you will certainly encounter a syntax error.

Ruby's Programming Mode
On the other hand, the programming mode is a method wherein you can execute blocks of code in one go. You will need to type the code of your program first before you can run and see what it will do.

You will need a text editor to type your program. Any simple text editor such as Notepad in Windows is sufficient for programming Ruby. However, to reduce typos and keyword mistakes, it is advisable that you use a source code editor, which will provide you with syntax highlighting and checking. In Windows users, a few of the best source code editors you can use for Ruby programming are Notepad++, TextWrangler, JEdit, and Crimson Editor.

Once you are done typing your code, save it as a .rb file. For Windows users: if you have let Ruby associate .rb and .rbw files to it, all .rb files or Ruby code you have created can be opened by just double clicking on them. They will act as if they are typical Windows program.

By the way, programming mode does not provide instant reply to your expressions. For example, if you input a = 1 + 1 in interactive mode, it will reply with => 2. In programming mode, that statement will not provide any output.

Also, if one of the lines encounters an error, the program will stop executing the next lines after the line that generated the error.

Chapter 2: Ruby Syntax

In the first chapter, you have encountered your first syntax error. For those who are not familiar with the term syntax, syntax is a set of 'language' rules that you must follow in order for a programming language (in this case, Ruby) to understand you.

A programming language's syntax is similar to English grammar where you need to correctly arrange parts of the sentence—such as verbs, nouns, and adjectives—to make it coherent and grammatically correct.

The two major differences between Ruby's syntax (or other programming languages' syntax as well) and English's set of grammar rules are Ruby's syntax's strictness and inflexibility. It is set to behave like that because computers, unlike humans, cannot understand or comprehend context. Also, if computers understand context and programming languages' syntaxes become lax, computer programming will become difficult.

First, computer will become prone to misunderstanding or misinterpreting your statements. If you point to a jar of jam in a shelf full of jars and requested people to get the one you want, most of them will surely get and give you the wrong jar. That kind of situation will happen if a programming language's syntax became loose.

Here are some of Ruby's syntax rules:

Whitespace

Whitespace (continuous spaces and tabs) are ignored in Ruby code unless they are placed inside strings. For example, the expression "1 + 1", "1 + 1", or 1+1 will provide the same result in Ruby.

Line Ending Terminators

New lines and semicolons are treated as line endings. Ruby works by reading your program's lines one by one. Each line is considered a statement. A statement is a combination of keywords, operators, values, methods, and properties, which is translated as a command.

Every time you put a semicolon or move to the next line, the previous line will be treated as a statement. There are some cases that if you do not place a semicolon but used a new line character (the one that the Enter key produces and pushes the cursor to move to the next line) to write a new line of code will make Ruby think that the previous line and the new line of code is just one statement. For example:

```
irb(main):001:0> 1 +
irb(main):002:0* 1 +
irb(main):003:0*
```

If you typed that in Ruby's interactive mode, you will not encounter an error or reply from Ruby. Instead, it allowed you to move on to the next line and type another line of code.

If you have noticed, the greater than sign at the end of the prompt changed into an asterisk. The asterisk denotes that all the succeeding lines of code after the previous one will be treated as one statement in Ruby or the next lines are meant to be continuations of the previous line.

Ruby behaved like that since you left an operator at the end of the line and did not place a value on the operator's right hand side. So, Ruby is treating the example as 1 + 1 +. If you place another 1 at the last line, Ruby will interpret that 1 as the last value to your expression and evaluate it. It will then produce a reply, which is => 3.

Case Sensitivity

Identifiers or names of constants, variables, and methods in Ruby are case sensitive. For example, a variable named Variable1 is different from variable1.

Comments

In computer languages, comments are used to serve as markers, reminders, or explanations within the program. Comments are ignored by Ruby and are not executed like regular statements.

Some convert statements in order to disable them. It is handy during debugging or testing alternate statements to get what they want since deleting a statement may make them forget it after a few minutes of coding another line.

To create comments in Ruby, use the hash sign (#) to let Ruby know that the succeeding characters is a comment line. You can insert comments at the end of statements. For example:

```
irb(main):001:0> #This is a comment.
irb(main):002:0* 1 + 1
=> 2
irb(main):003:0> 1 + 1 #This is a comment.
=> 2
irb(main):003:0>
```

As you can see, the line after the hash sign was just ignored and Ruby just evaluated the expression 1 + 1.

In case you are going to start programming using Ruby's programming mode, there will be times that you will want to create multiple lines of comments. You can still use hash signs to create multiple lines. For example:

```
#This is a comment.
#This is another comment.
#This is the last comment.
```

If you do not want to use that method, you can do this by using the =begin and =end keyword. Below is an example on how to use them:

```
=begin
This is a comment
This is another comment.
This is the last comment.
=end
```

All lines after the =begin and before the =end keyword will be treated as comment lines.

Those are just the primary rules in Ruby's syntax. Some commands have syntax of their own. They will be discussed together with the commands themselves.

Chapter 3: Parts of a Statement

You have been seeing the term statement in the previous chapters. As mentioned before, a statement is a combination of keywords, operators, variables, constants, values, expressions, methods, and properties which is translated as a command.
In this chapter, you will know what six of those parts are: variables, constants, keywords, values, operators, and expressions. Let's start with variables.

Variables

In Math, you know that variables are placeholders for values. For example:
x = 1 + 1
x = 2
y = 3
In the previous line, variable x has a value of 2 and variable y has a value of 3. Variables in Ruby (or other programming languages) act the same way – as placeholders. However, unlike in Math, variables in Ruby do not act as placeholders for numbers alone. It can contain different types of values like strings and objects.
To create variables in Ruby, all you need is to assign a value to one. For example:
irb(main):001:0> a = 12

That example commands Ruby to create a variable named a and assign the number 12 as its value. To check the value of a variable in Ruby's interpreter mode, input a on a new line and press the Enter key. It will produce the result:
=> 12

A while ago, instead of getting a reply like that from Ruby, you have got this instead:
NameError: undefined local variable or method 'a' for main:Object
        from (irb):1
        from C:/Ruby21/bin/irb:11:in '<main>'

Technically, the error means that Ruby was not able to find a variable or method with the name a. Now, when you input a, it does not produce that error anymore since you have already created a variable named a.
By the name, in computer programming, the names you give to variables and other entities in the program are called identifiers. Some call them IDs or tokens instead.
There are some set of rules when giving an identifier to a variable. Identifiers can contain letters, numbers, and underscores. A variable identifier must start with a lower case letter or an underscore. It may also contain one or more characters. Also, variable identifiers should not be the same with a keyword or reserved words.
Just like any programming languages, reserved or special keywords cannot be used as identifiers.

Constants

Constants are like variables, but you can only assign a value to them once in your program and their identifiers must start with an uppercase letter. Reassigning a value to them will generate an error or a warning.

Keywords

Keywords are special reserved words in Ruby that perform specific functions and commands. Some of them are placeholder for special values such as true, false, and nil.

The nil value means that the entity that contains it does not have a value. To put it simply, all variables will have the nil value if no value was assigned to it. When they are used and they have nil as their value, Ruby will return a warning if the – w is on.

Values

In Ruby, there are multiple types of values that you can assign in a variable. In programming, they are called literals. In coding Ruby, you will be dealing with these literals every time.

Integers

You can write integers in four forms or numeral systems: decimal, hexadecimal, octal, and binary. To make Ruby understand that you are declaring integers in hexadecimal (base 16), octal (base 8), or binary (base 2), you should use prefixes or leading signs.

If you are going to use octal, use 0 (zero). If you are going to use hexadecimal, use 0x (zero-x). If you are going to use binary, use 0b (zero-b). If you are going to use decimal, there is no need for any optional leading signs.

Depending on the size of the integer, it can be categorized in the class Fixnum or Bignum.

Floating Numbers

Any integer with decimals is considered a floating number. All floating numbers are under the class Float.

Strings

Strings are values inside single or double quotation marks. They are treated as text in Ruby. You can place expression evaluation inside strings without terminating your quotes. You can just insert expressions by using the hash sign and enclosing the expression using curly braces. For example:
irb(main):001:0> a = "the sum of 3 and 1 is: #{3 + 1}."
=> "the sum of 3 and 1 is: 4."

You can also access variables or constants in Ruby and include them in a string by placing a hash sign (#) before the variable or constant's name. For example:
irb(main):001:0> b = "string inside variable."

=> "string inside variable."
irb(main):002:0> b = "You can access a #{b}"
=> "You can access a string inside variable."

Arrays

An array is a data type that can contain multiple data or values. Creating arrays in Ruby is simple. Type Array and then follow it with values enclosed inside square brackets. Make sure that you separate each value with a comma. Any exceeding commas will be ignored and will not generate error. For example:
irb(main):001:0> arraysample = Array[1, 2, 3]
=> [1, 2, 3]

To access a value of an array, you must use its index. The index of an array value depends on its location in the array. For example, the value 2 in the arraysample variable has an index number of 0. The value 2, has an index of 1. And the value 3, has an index of 2. The index increments by 1 and starts with zero.
Below is an example on how to access a value in an array:
irb(main):001:0> arraysample[2]
=> 3

Hashes or Associative Arrays:

Hashes are arrays that contain paired keys (named index) and values. Instead of a numbered index, you can assign and use keys to access your array values.
irb(main):001:0> hashsample = Hash["First" => 1, "Second" = > 2]
=> {"First"=>1, "Second"=>2]

To access a hash value, you just need to call it using its key instead of an index number. For example:
irb(main):001:0> hashsample["Second"]
=> 2

Expressions

Expressions are combinations of operators, variables, values, and/or keywords. Expressions result into a value or can be evaluated by Ruby. A good example of an expression is 1 + 1. In that, Ruby can evaluate that expression and it will result to 2. The plus sign (+) is one of many operators in Ruby.
You can assign expression to a variable. The result of the expression will be stored on the variable instead of the expression itself. For example:
irb(main):001:0> a = 1 + 1
=> 2

If you check the value of a by inputting a into the shell, it will return 2 not 1 + 1.

As mentioned a while ago, expressions can also contain variables. If you assign a simple or complex expression with a variable to another variable, Ruby will handle all the evaluation. For example:
irb(main):001:0> a = 2
=> 2
irb(main):002:0> b = 4
=> 4
irb(main):003:0> c = a + b + 6
=> 12

Operators

Operators are symbols or keywords that command the computer to perform operations or evaluations. Ruby's operators are not limited to performing arithmetic operations alone. The following are the operators you can use in Ruby:

Arithmetic Operators

Arithmetic operators allow Ruby to evaluate simple Math expressions. They are: + for addition, - for subtraction, * for multiplication, / for division, % for modulus, and ** for exponent.
Division in Ruby works differently. If you are dividing integers, you will get an integer quotient. If the quotient should have a fractional component or decimal on it, they will be removed. For example:
irb(main):001:0> 5 / 2
=> 2

If you want to get an accurate quotient with a fractional component, you must perform division with fractional components For example:
irb(main):001:0> 5.0 / 2
=> 2.5

For those who are unfamiliar with modulus: modulus performs regular division and returns the remainder instead of the quotient. For example:
irb(main):001:0> 5 % 2
=> 1

Comparison Operators

Ruby can compare numbers, too, with the help of comparison operators. Comparison operations provide two results only: true or false. For example:
irb(main):001:0> 1 > 2
=> false

The value 1 is less than 2, but not greater than; therefore, Ruby evaluated that the expression is false.
Other comparison operators that you can use in Ruby are: == for has equal value, != for does not have equal value, > for greater than, < for less than, >= for greater

than or equal, and <= for less than or equal. There four other comparison operators (===, <=>, .eql?, and .equal?) in Ruby, but you do not need them for now.

Assignment Operators

Assignment operators are used to assign value to operators, properties, and other entities in Ruby. You have already encountered the most used assignment operator, which is the equal sign (=). There are other assignment operators other than that, which are simple combination of the assignment operator (=) and arithmetic operators.

They are += for add and assign, -= for subtract and assign, *= for multiply and assign, /= for divide and assign, % for modulus and assign, and ** for raise and assign.

All of them perform the arithmetic operation and the values they use are the value of the entity on their left and the expression on their right first before assigning the result of the operation to the entity on its left. It might seem confusing, so here is an example:

irb(main):001:0> a = 1
=> 1
irb(main):002:0> a += 2
=> 3

In the example, variable a was given a value of 1. On the next statement, the add and assign operator was used. After the operation, a's value became 3 because a + 2 = 3. That can also be achieved by doing this:

irb(main):001:0> a = 1
=> 1
irb(main):002:0> a = a + 2
=> 3

If the value to the right of these operators is an expression that contain multiple values and operators, it will be evaluated first before the assignment operators perform their operations. For example:

irb(main):001:0> a = 1
=> 1
irb(main):002:0> a += 3 * 2
=> 7

The expression 3 * 2 was evaluated first, which resulted to 6. Then six was added to variable a that had a value of 1, which resulted to 7. And that value value was assigned to variable a.

Other Operators

As you advance your Ruby programming skills, you will encounter more operators. And they are:

Logical Operator: and, or, &&, ||, !, not

Defined Operator: defined?

Reference Operators: ., ::

Chapter 4: Object Oriented Programming

In the previous chapters, you have learned the basics of Ruby programming. Those chapters also serve as your introduction to computer programming since most programming languages follow the same concepts and have similar entities in them. In this chapter, you will learn why some programmers love Ruby.

Ruby is an Object Oriented Programming (OOP) language. Object oriented programming makes use of objects and classes. Those objects and classes can be reused which in turn makes it easier to code programs that require multiple instances of values that are related to each other.

Programming methods can be categorized into two: Procedural and Object Oriented. If you have experienced basic programming before, you mostly have experienced procedural instead of object oriented.

In procedural, your program's code revolves around actions. For example, you have a program that prints what a user will input. It is probable that your program's structure will be as simple as take user input, assign the input to a variable, and then print the content of the variable. As you can see, procedural is a straightforward forward method.

Classes and Objects

Classes are like templates for objects. For example, a Fender Telecaster and a Gibson Les Paul are objects and they are under the electric guitar class.

In programming, you can call those guitars as instances of the class of objects named electric guitars. Each object has its own properties or characteristics.

Objects under the same class have same properties, but the value of those properties may differ or be the same per object. For example, think that an electric guitar's properties are: brand, number of strings, and number of guitar pickups.

Aside from that, each object has its own functions or things that it can do. When it comes to guitars, you can strum all the strings or you can just pick on one string.

If you convert that to Ruby code, that will appear as:

```
class ElectricGuitar
        def initialize
                @brand = "Local"
                @strings = 6
                @pickups = 3
        end
        def strum
                #Insert statements to execute when strum is called
        end
        def pick
                #Insert statements to execute when strum is called
end
```

Creating a Class

To create a class, you need to use the class keyword and an identifier. Class identifiers have the same syntax rules for constant identifiers. To end the creation of the class, you need to use the end keyword. For example:

```
irb(main):001:0> class Guitar
irb(main):002:1> end
=> nil
```

Creating an Object

Now, you have a class. It is time for you to create an object. To create one, all you need is to think of an identifier and assign the class name and the keyword new to it for it to become an object under a class. For example:

```
irb(main):001:0> fender = Guitar. new
=> #<Guitar:0x1234567>
```

Note: Do not forget to add a dot operator after the class name.
Unfortunately, the class Guitar does not contain anything in it. That object is still useless and cannot be used for anything. To make it useful, you need to add some methods and properties to it.

Methods

This is where it gets interesting. Methods allow your objects to have 'commands' of some sort. In case you want to have multiple lines of statements to be done, placing them under a class method is the best way to do that. To give your classes or objects methods, you will need to use the def (define) keyword. Below is an example:

```
irb(main):001:0> class Guitar
irb(main):002:1> def strum
irb(main):003:2> puts "Starts strumming."
irb(main):004:2> puts "Strumming."
irb(main):005:2> puts "Ends strumming."
irb(main):006:2> end
irb(main):007:1> end
=> :strum
```

Now, create a new object under that class.

```
irb(main):008:0> gibson = Guitar. new
=> #<Guitar:0x1234567>
```

To use the method you have created, all you need is to invoke it using the object. For example:

```
irb(main):009:0> gibson.strum
Starts strumming.
Strumming.
Ends strumming.
=> nil
```

By using the dot operator, you were able to invoke the method inside the gibson object under the Guitar class. All the objects that will be under Guitar class will be able to use that method.

Conclusion

Thank you again for purchasing this book!
I hope this book was able to help you understand how coding in Ruby works.
The next step is to:

- Learn more about flow control tools in Ruby

- Study about the other operators discussed in this book

- Research on how variables inside classes and objects work

Finally, if you enjoyed this book, please take the time to share your thoughts and post a review on Amazon. We do our best to reach out to readers and provide the best value we can. Your positive review will help us achieve that. It'd be greatly appreciated!
Thank you and good luck!

Check Out My Other Books

Below you'll find some of my other popular books that are popular on Amazon and Kindle as well. Simply click on the links below to check them out. Alternatively, you can visit my author page on Amazon to see other work done by me.

C Programming Success in a Day

Python Programming Success in a Day

PHP Programming Professional Made Easy

HTML Professional Programming Made Easy

CSS Programming Professional Made Easy

Windows 8 Tips for Beginners

C Programming Professional Made Easy

JavaScript Programming Made Easy

Rails Programming Professional Made Easy

C ++ Programming Success in a Day

If the links do not work, for whatever reason, you can simply search for these titles on the Amazon website to find them.